Editor
Walter Kelly, M.A.

Editorial Project Manager
Ina Massler Levin, M.A.

Editor in Chief
Sharon Coan, M.S. Ed.

Illustrator
Agi Palinay

Cover Artists
Sue Fullam
José L. Tapia

Art Coordinator
Cheri Macoubrie Wilson

Associate Designer
Denise Bauer

Creative Director
Elayne Roberts

Imaging
James E. Grace

Product Manager
Phil Garcia

Publishers:
Rachelle Cracchiolo, M.S. Ed.
Mary Dupuy Smith, M.S. Ed.

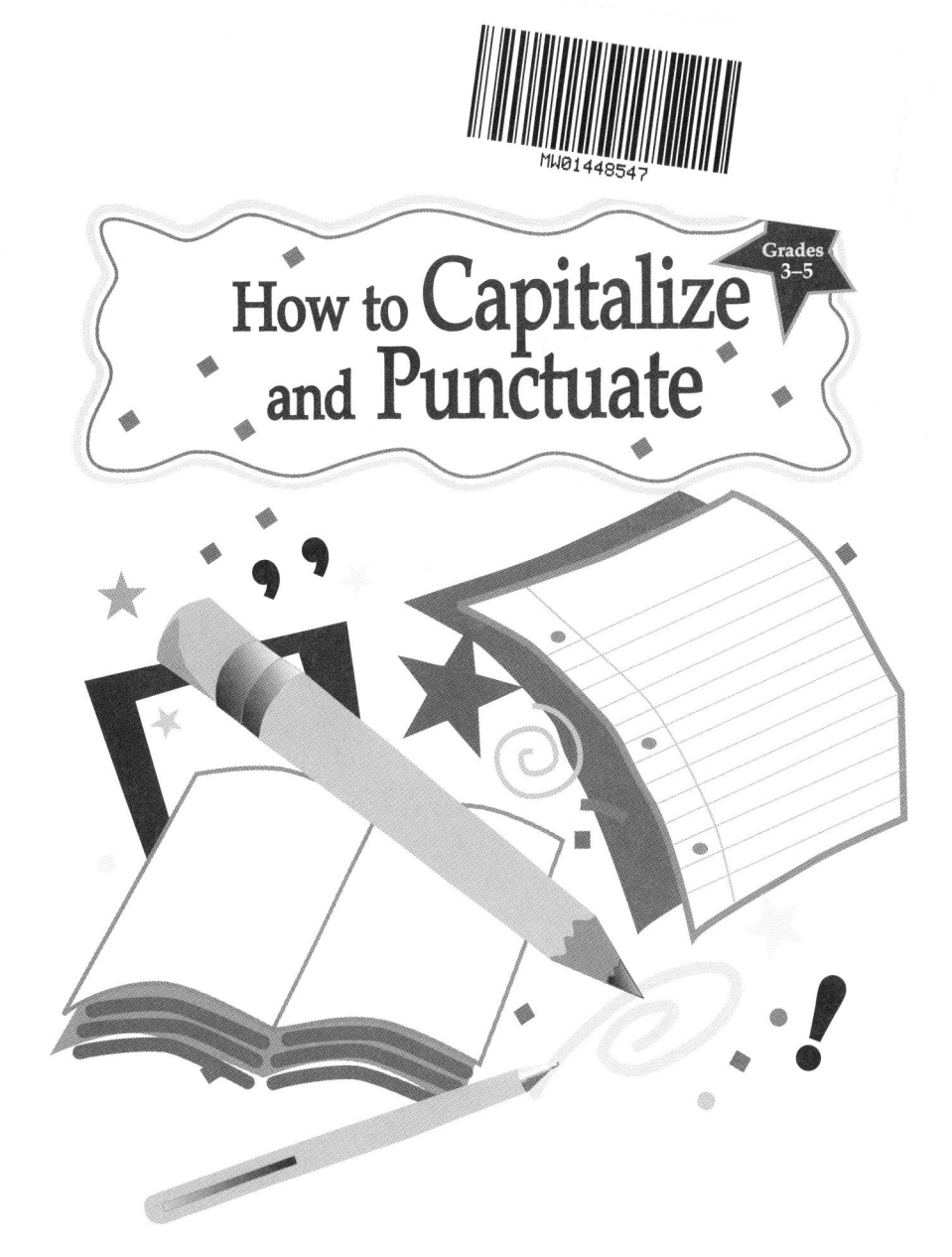

How to Capitalize and Punctuate

Grades 3–5

Author:

Kathleen Christopher Null

Teacher Created Materials, Inc.
6421 Industry Way
Westminster, CA 92683
www.teachercreated.com
ISBN-1-57690-329-X

©*1998 Teacher Created Materials, Inc.*
Reprinted, 2000
Made in U.S.A.

The classroom teacher may reproduce copies of materials in this book for classroom use only. The reproduction of any part for an entire school or school system is strictly prohibited. No part of this publication may be transmitted, stored, or reproduced in any form without written permission from the publisher.

Table of Contents

Introduction 3
Capitalization
    When and Why to Capitalize 4
    The Capital *I* 5
    What's in a Name? 7
    Titles and Abbreviations 9
    Days, Months, and Holidays 11
    Capital Places 13
    Sentences 15
    It's All Relative 16
    Subjects, Organizations, and Everything Else 18
    Capital Art 19
    Review 21
    Capital Game 22

Punctuation
    When and Why to Punctuate 24
    End Marks 29
    Abbreviations 31
    Contractions 32
    That's Mine! 34
    When and Where? 35
    Where's My List? 36
    Set It Off! 37
    May I Quote You? 39
    What Are These Funny Little Marks? 41
    Punctuate This! 42

Capitalization and Punctuation Review 43
Capitalization and Punctuation Posters 44
Answer Key 46

Introduction

The Basics...

The basics of capitalization and punctuation are essential to clear communication. This book presents these basics in a variety of ways. It begins with a section on capitalization which is followed by a section on punctuation.

The Sections...

Each of these sections begins with a "When and Why..." primer that can be utilized in any number of ways. You may wish to make copies for students to keep in their notebooks as a quick-reference handbook. These pages might also be used as a bulletin board display or laminated and placed in a writing center.

The Details...

More detailed information on capitalization and punctuation follows in each section along with plenty of activities for practicing the concepts being learned.

The Reinforcement...

Each section also includes an art activity and a game to reinforce learning in ways that are both enjoyable and adaptable to different learning styles.

The Assessment...

After completing both sections, students have an opportunity to edit a story for both capitalization and punctuation errors. Students may not even be aware that you are testing their skills as they revise the story. If you wish, you may use the story at the beginning of the year to assess abilities. Use it again to assess progress.

The Posters...

The book concludes with posters that will enhance learning with clever visuals that can also serve as reminders if posted in the classroom. These can be enlarged and colored if you wish, and/or copies may be distributed to students for their writing notebooks. Also, the examples appearing on pages 44 and 45 will serve as ideas for students to create their own posters illustrating correct punctuation. Encouraging such activity will aid understanding and retention of punctuation skills.

Capitalization

When and Why to Capitalize

The Basics in a Nutshell

To capitalize, you begin a word with a capital letter. Here is a list of the things you should always capitalize.

- **the word *I***
  At the fair I bought a balloon.
- **the first word in a sentence**
  My dog doesn't like the rain.
- **the names of people and places**
  (proper nouns)
  James   Eiffel Tower
  San Francisco Germany
- **words derived from proper nouns**
  (proper adjectives)
  German   New Yorker
  African   Texan
- **titles with people's names**
  (titles of position, rank, etc.)
  Dr. William   Mrs. Hernandez
  Captain Ross   President Eisenhower
- **title** (of a person) when used in place of that person's name.
  Thank you, Doctor. You're very helpful.
  (*Family members also have "titles" which should be capitalized when they are used as part of a name or in place of a name.*)
  This is Uncle Bob. I told Grandma I would come see her.
- **days of the week and months**
  Sunday Monday Tuesday Wednesday
  Thursday Friday Saturday
  January February March April May
  June July August September
  October November December
- **the first word in a letter to a friend or relative**
  Dear Janny,   Dear Friends,
- **the first letter of each word in a business letter greeting**
  To Whom It May Concern: Dear Students:

- **the main words** (usually all words except *prepositions, conjunctions,* or *the, an* and *a*) **in titles of books, movies, newspapers, television shows, plays, operas, musicals, or magazines** (These titles need to be in italics or underlined.)
  A Wrinkle in Time
  The Los Angeles Times
  Phantom of the Opera
- **school subjects if they are languages or actual class titles listed in a catalog**
  Italian   Modern American Art
  Women Inventors   Algebra I
- **geographic locations when they name specific areas**
  He lived in the East all his life.
  She wrote about the South.
- **holidays**
  Labor Day   Fourth of July   Cinco de Mayo
  Garlic Festival   Memorial Day
  Passover   Christmas

Here are some times when you should **not** capitalize.

- **persons' titles when not used with a name or in place of a name**
  My mother told me to call the doctor.
  The president went to the same school that my dad attended.
- **the four seasons**
  winter spring summer autumn *or* fall
- **regular school subjects**
  mathematics   history   social studies
- **geographical directions**
  We decided to head west.
  Go north along Campfire Street.

Capitalization

The Capital *I*

When you write about yourself, you can use the word *I*. **The word *I* is always capitalized no matter where it is found in a sentence.** The word *I* is a proper pronoun that takes the place of your name. Imagine how you would write if you did not have the capitalized word *I*. Here is how Leticia would write:

> My name is Leticia and Leticia lives on Waterlily Lane. Leticia likes to play with my friends until my mom calls me in for dinner. After dinner Leticia clears the table. Then Leticia does my homework.

It sounds kind of strange, doesn't it? The word *I* is very important.

In the sentences below, use the proofreader's mark (≡) to show where the word *I* needs to be capitalized. The first one has been done for you.

1. I stayed at the game longer than *i* thought *i* would.

2. It was late when i got home.

3. i was surprised that there were no lights on.

4. i wondered where my family was.

5. The door pushed open as i started to put my key in the lock.

6. i was scared, so i turned to leave.

7. Then i heard footsteps in the kitchen.

8. A hand reached out and grabbed me, and i screamed!

9. "Surprise! Happy Birthday!" i saw many friends and relatives looking at me while i sat on the floor.

10. That was a birthday party i will never forget!

Extension: Try writing a story about something that happened to you without using the word "I."

Capitalization

The Capital *I* *(cont.)*

Insert the missing words in each rainbow sentence and lightly color each band with the color used in the sentence.
Remember: Always capitalize the word *I*.

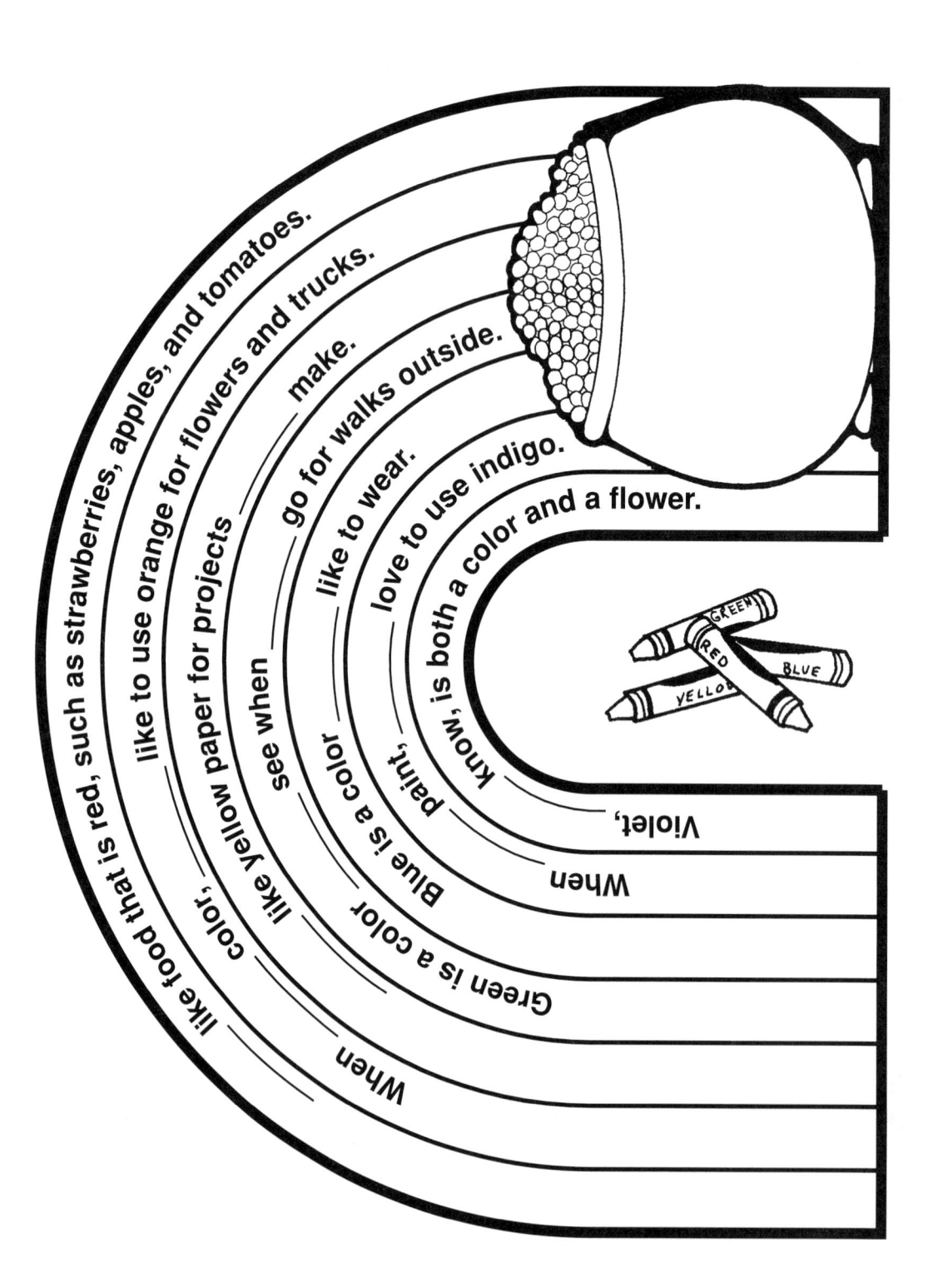

When ____ like food that is red, such as strawberries, apples, and tomatoes.
____ like to use orange for flowers and trucks.
____ color.
____ like yellow paper for projects ____ make.
Green is a color ____ see when ____ go for walks outside.
Blue is a color ____ like to wear.
____ paint, ____ love to use indigo.
When ____ know, Violet, is both a color and a flower.

#2329 How to Capitalize and Punctuate

Capitalization

What's in a Name?

Did you know that your name is a proper noun? It is, and **you should always capitalize your first and last names and middle name if you have one**. And what about your pet snake? If you call your snake "George", "Rex," or "Samantha Slither," you should capitalize that, too. And if your stuffed animal is named "Old MacDonald" that name should be capitalized, with the M of Mac (or Mc) capitalized and the D of Donald also capitalized. Your little brother has the nickname, "Punkin"? That would also be capitalized. I think you get the picture.

Rewrite the following names so that they are properly capitalized.

amanda panda _____

jeffrey r. hardy _____

carlos custard appleseed _____

gilbert mcgillicutty _____

leslie q. presley _____

Do you have any pets at home? If you do, write the names of your pets (or any other pets you know) here.

_____
_____
_____
_____

Here are some pets without names. Think of a name for each pet. The names can be fancy or simple, long or short, but they should all be capitalized. The first one has been done as an example.

Malcolm Angus McCollie McDuff   _____   _____   _____

Extension: Make a *Names Notebook*. In a small notebook, write all the creative names you can think of in alphabetical order. Be sure to capitalize! Keep your notebook handy. The next time you write a story, you will have lots of interesting names from which to choose.

© Teacher Created Materials, Inc.   7   #2329 How to Capitalize and Punctuate

Capitalization

What's in a Name? *(cont.)*

Each year the students at Wiggleworm School have a pet day. On pet day each student is allowed to bring a pet to school to share. Usually things go pretty well, but this year things got a little out of hand. In this story about the pet show, draw a line through each letter that needs to be capitalized and write the capital letter above it.

Pet Day at Wiggleworm Elementary School

mrs. wolfe was in charge, and she stood at the entrance of wiggleworm elementary school to welcome the students. lindsay harper entered first with her goldfish named twitty. Next came lorenzo lopez with a cat, fang. fang scratched lorenzo and tried to get a bite of the goldfish, twitty. When samantha rissota arrived with her big, shaggy dog named crackers, crackers immediately took off after fang, the cat, dragging samantha behind as she held fast to the leash. As samantha went flying by, she accidentally knocked over jacob fritz and his ant farm. The ant farm broke, and thousands of ants began to crawl away. "doc, loretta, steve and darlene, licorice, pepper—come back!" jacob knelt over the ants and pleaded with them to return. Just then, fibber, tasha armstrong's parrot, landed next to the ants and looked at them with great interest. "fibber!" tasha cried and raced across the room to tackle her parrot. The parrot flew to perch on the light fixtures, and tasha flew into jonny mcandrew, who was carrying two pet frogs, antony and cleopatra. The frogs hopped away slowly and then more quickly as they realized they were being chased by fang the cat. fang the cat was being chased by crackers the dog, and lindsay harper was trying to get her goldfish, twitty, back into the bowl, but she was too slippery. mrs. wolfe was trying to remove the ants that were crawling on her when she saw victoria pleasant arriving with her snake, priscilla, and jake jasso coming up behind victoria with his pet monkey, billie. mrs. wolfe, scratching her arms and legs, blocked the doorway, which surprised victoria, priscilla, jake, and billie. "Stop! You're too late. Pet day is over. This was the last pet day ever, and you may go home now. Try not to be late for school tomorrow!" victoria, with priscilla wrapped around her neck, smiled and skipped home. When jake peeked in the window to the classroom, he saw that mrs. wolfe was clapping her hands and saying, "Now class! It's a short day today; you may go home now!"

Extension: Illustrate the story. It might help if you make a list of all the pets and their owners first. Be sure to capitalize all their names.

Capitalization

Titles and Abbreviations

Here is how to capitalize the title of a book, a movie, a play, a magazine, a work of art, or a newspaper. Capitalize the first word, the last word, and every word in between except for *a, an, the*, short prepositions, and short conjunctions. Then underline the title or put it all in capital letters. If you have a computer or word processor, italicize the title. Here are some title examples.

The Wizard of Oz (book)
The New York Times (newspaper)
Reader's Digest (magazine)
The Wind in the Willows (book)
Beauty and the Beast (movie)

Return of the Jedi (movie)
Boys' Life (magazine)
Walking Quickly Under the Rain (sculpture)
Once Upon a Mattress (play)
Mona Lisa (painting)

Here is how to capitalize a poem, a song, an article, a work of art, a picture, a story, or an essay. Capitalize the first word, the last word, and every word in between except for *a, an, the*, short prepositions, and short conjunctions, just as you do for titles of books, movies, plays, magazines, or newspapers. There is a difference, however: with poems, songs, articles, pictures, stories and essays, you do not underline, italicize, or put the titles in all capitals. Instead, you use quotation marks. Here are some examples:

"I Want to Hold Your Hand" (song)
"Picture-Books in Winter" (poem)
"For Emily, Whenever I May Find Her" (song)
"Time to Rise" (poem)
"The Dance at the Gym" (musical piece)
"The Grasshopper and the Ants" (story)

"I Have a Dream" (speech)
"New York Child" (photograph)
"Why Frog and Snake Never Play Together" (story)
"Emerson on Friendship" (essay)
"So Proud of Her Father" (article)

Abbreviations are everywhere, and it is a good thing, too. If you are writing a mystery story that has a part about the Federal Bureau of Investigation, you won't have to write it out after the first time. Instead, you can write FBI in capitals. That's much better, isn't it? If your teacher has a Master of Arts degree, he or she does not need to write it that way when applying for a job to teach your class. He or she can simply write M.A.

If your name is Samuel and your dad is also named Samuel, your name can use an abbreviation too: Samuel, Jr. Here are some more abbreviations:

Mr. = Mister
Ph.D. = Doctor of Philosophy
Miss = Mistress
Dr. = Doctor
NATO = North Atlantic Treaty Organization
M.D. = Medical Doctor
U.S.A. = United States of America
Capt. = Captain

PTA = Parent Teacher Association
NFL = National Football League
NASA = National Aeronautics and Space Administration
CIA = Central Intelligence Agency
BMW = Bavarian Motor Works
JPL = Jet Propulsion Lab

Capitalization

Titles and Abbreviations *(cont.)*

Get out your editor's pen and edit the following article. Pay special attention to titles and abbreviations. But watch out, there may be a few more capitalization errors that need to be corrected. Use the proofreader's mark for *capitalize* (≡) under the letter that needs to be capitalized. Also, underline the titles that need italics and place quotation marks where they are needed.

what people are Seeing

There are many hardworking people in our part of the u.s.a., and our busy reporters set out to discover what these hard workers do for entertainment when it's time to take a break. first we asked dr. lewis s. chimney what movie he saw last weekend. this is what dr. chimney had to say, "As an emergency room doctor, i really don't need to see any more accidents or messy injuries, so i stay away from violent movies." Last weekend he rented mary poppins. he said his favorite song in the movie is chim, chim-cheree. "The chimney sweeps," he added, "are the best!"

Lyle m. sewsmith, m.d., said that he spent his one day off last week at the art museum. "I really like the Van Gogh section," dr. sewsmith said. his favorite van gogh painting is titled starry night. a plastic surgeon, dr. sewsmith spent a long time studying van gogh's self-portrait.

mrs. d.l. cleat, a busy school teacher, went to a sculpture garden on her way to a baseball game on Saturday. She said that she saw a version of the thinker, a sculpture by Rodin. "I wish all my students would think that hard," she commented. At the ball game she sang take me out to the ball game along with all the fans.

jan l. mcjet, ph.d, a scientist at jpl, took her kids, miranda, mark, jr., and misha to see the magic flute. "It was very nice," she said, "but the youngest, misha, got bored and started to cry." Where was mr. mcjet on this sunny saturday? "He's at a pta convention. We miss him!"

jason nurdberry, a student, said that he spent his weekend writing a story. "It's about a guy who wants to join the cia. the only problem is that he's just 12 years old, but he's really smart and would do a great job. He spends all his time trying to prove to them how much they need him. I got the idea from an article about the cia in reader's digest."

so it is that the very busy people around here are also busy on the weekends. what we have learned from these hard workers gives new meaning to the phrase, "Thank goodness it's friday!" (TGIF).

Extension: Write a story using as many abbreviations as you can. You might want to research first, using reference volumes at the library (ask a librarian if you need help). Make a list of as many abbreviation as you can find and then see how many you can incorporate into a short story.

Capitalization

Days, Months, and Holidays

What day of the week is today? _____

Did you use a capital letter to begin your answer? If you did, you used a capitalization rule.

What month of the year is today? _____

Did you use a capital letter to begin your answer? If you did, you used a capitalization rule again!

What is your favorite holiday? _____

Did you use a capital to start? If you did, you know the rules for capitalizing days, months, and holidays!

- ❏ Always capitalize **the days of the week.**
- ❏ Always capitalize **the months of the year.**
- ❏ Always capitalize **the names of holidays**.

That should be easy to remember. Now for some practice.

Here is a days-of-the-week watch for you to color and put on the wrist of a younger child when you teach him or her the days of the week.

Put these words in order on the watch face and capitalize them (start with Sunday).

- friday
- wednesday
- sunday
- tuesday
- monday
- saturday
- thursday

Color the watch, cut it out, and attach to a strap of Velcro. Place a small paper clip on the correct day of the week and change it the next morning.

List the months of the year in order on the the lines. Don't forget to capitalize! Next to each month, write what you like best about that month.

- january
- february
- march
- october
- may
- june
- august
- september
- april
- november
- december
- july

1. _____ 7. _____
2. _____ 8. _____
3. _____ 9. _____
4. _____ 10. _____
5. _____ 11. _____
6. _____ 12. _____

Extension: With 12 large sheets of construction paper folded in half widthwise, create your own calendar. Put art on the top half of each piece of paper and the monthly calendar on the bottom half (you can create these items on white paper and glue them onto the construction paper). Be sure to capitalize all the months and days of the week.

Capitalization

Days, Months, and Holidays *(cont.)*

There are some names of holidays on this page. They are not capitalized correctly. Capitalize the holidays by changing a lowercase letter to a capital letter where it is needed. As you write each capital letter, color the same letter in the heart.

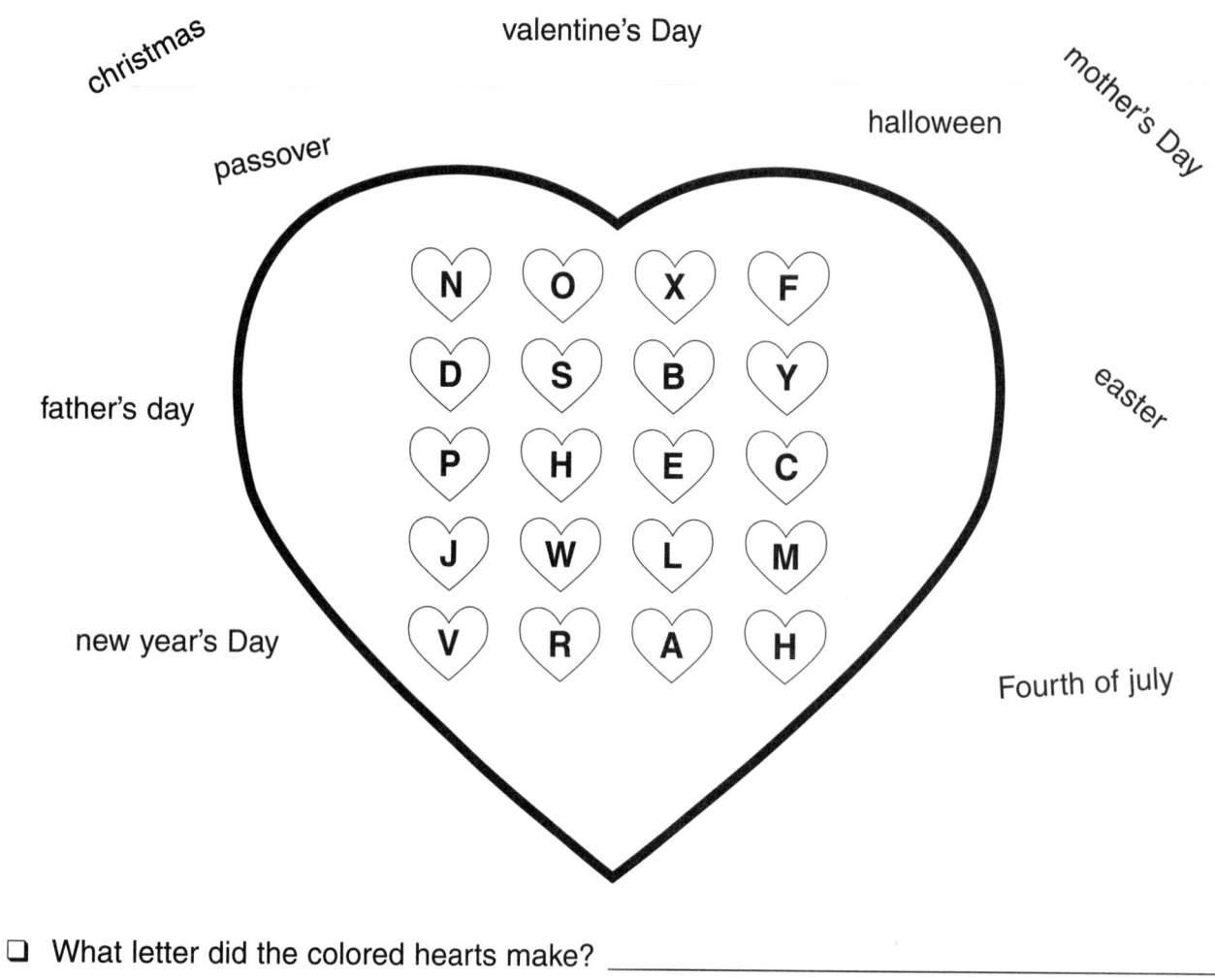

christmas

valentine's Day

passover

halloween

mother's Day

father's day

N	O	X	F
D	S	B	Y
P	H	E	C
J	W	L	M
V	R	A	H

easter

new year's Day

Fourth of july

- ❑ What letter did the colored hearts make? _____
- ❑ Write the names of two holidays that begin with this letter.
    1. _____
    2. _____
- ❑ Color the rest of the heart!

#2329 How to Capitalize and Punctuate © Teacher Created Materials, Inc.

Capitalization

Capital Places

Here are some more things that always begin with capital letters.

- **Street Names**
  - Rabbit's Foot Lane
  - Watermelon Avenue
  - Awesome Circle
- **Cities**
  - San Francisco
  - London
  - Little Rock
- **States and Provinces**
  - Montana
  - Quebec
  - New Mexico
- **Countries**
  - New Zealand
  - Canada
  - Italy
- **Continents**
  - South America
  - Asia
  - Europe
- **Oceans**
  - Pacific Ocean
  - Adriatic Sea
  - North Sea

- **Rivers**
  - Mississippi River
  - Amazon River
  - Jordan River
- **Lakes**
  - Lake Victoria
  - Lake Tahoe
  - Lake Superior
- **Islands**
  - Borneo
  - Hawaiian Islands
  - Cyprus
- **Canyons**
  - Grand Canyon
  - Bryce Canyon
  - Canyon de Chelly
- **Mountains**
  - Mount Everest
  - Himalayas
  - Mount Kilimanjaro
- **Buildings**
  - Eiffel Tower
  - Empire State Building
  - British Museum

The proper names of all geographical locations are capitalized. Can you think of any others? How about **creeks**, **streams**, **malls**, **parks**, **ponds**, **campgrounds**, **dams**, **reservoirs**, **coves**, **beaches**, **towns**, **peninsulas**, **estuaries**, **gardens**, **waterfalls**, **cliffs**, **points**, **bays**, **harbors**, **bridges**, **trails**, **villages**, **volcanoes**, and **geysers**?

Extension: List your continent, country, state or province, city or town, and street. Be sure to capitalize! Think of an example of each of the geographic locations above, including waterfalls, malls, dams, etc., and list them.

© Teacher Created Materials, Inc.   13   #2329 *How to Capitalize and Punctuate*

Capitalization

Capital Places *(cont.)*

It's vacation time!

Do you like to go to museums, zoos, or parks? _____

Do you like to travel to lakes, oceans, rivers, or mountains? _____

These and other places need capital letters.

Here is a list of places that need capital letters. Write the capital letters that are needed. Then choose three of the places you would like to visit.

pacific ocean	sahara desert	rocky Mountains
Grand canyon	North pole	hyde park
Mt. rushmore	san diego zoo	disneyland
amazon River	lake Louise	niagara falls

I would like to go to . . .

1. _____
2. _____
3. _____

In the space below, draw one of the places you chose. Tell the class why you would like to go there as you show your picture.

Capitalization

Sentences

One of the most important capitalization rules is also one of the easiest to remember. **Always capitalize the first word of every sentence**. It doesn't matter whether the word is *I, you, me, Clara the Clown, Africa, a, the,* or *nerds*, the first word of every sentence is always capitalized. It doesn't matter whether it is a word that is normally capitalized or not.

Let's see how you do. In the story below, there are some words that need to be capitalized. Use a colored pencil or pen to write the capital letter above the letter that is there.

❑ ❑ ❑

one day, Mike and Chris were riding their skateboards at the park. when they stopped to rest, they noticed something in the bushes. "what is that?" Chris asked. mike looked more closely. "it's furry!" Mike said. both boys stood and stared, and then they saw it move just a little bit.

"ohhh," Chris said, "that scared me!"

"it's a little bunny!" Mike exclaimed. sure enough, it was a scared little brown bunny hiding in the bushes. mike and chris cornered it, and then mike scooped it up. he could feel its heart beating very rapidly.

the boys walked around the park asking people if they lost a bunny. nobody claimed it, so Mike and Chris took it home.

mike sat in a chair watching TV and held the bunny close to his chest. chris made telephone calls to try to find out who had lost the bunny. next, they made signs and put them up around the park and in the neighborhood. the signs said, "Lost Bunny," and gave their telephone number. no one claimed the bunny.

"you can't keep it," Chris and Mike's dad said.

"why not?" Chris asked.

"we already have a bunny cage," Mike added.

"well, okay," Dad said, "but you'll have to give it food and water every day."

the boys were happy. they named the rabbit "George," even though it was a girl rabbit. they fed her all the vegetable scraps from the kitchen—rabbit food, cabbage, dandelions, and water. george grew to be a big fat rabbit who would sometimes visit the neighbor's yards to eat weeds and dandelions which are, to this day, her favorite foods.

Extension: Divide into teams and see which team can mark the capitals the fastest with the most accuracy.

Capitalization

It's All Relative

Do you have aunts, uncles, grandmothers, grandfather, moms, dads, and cousins? If you do, this information is for you.

Did you notice how all those words (*aunts, uncles*, etc.) were **not** capitalized? Usually those words are not capitalized. If you say "I have 13 cousins, and none of them looks like me," you do not capitalize the word *cousins*. But there are two times when you would.

1. You capitalize when using the word *cousin* as a title.

    "I would like you to meet Cousin Ruth."

2. You capitalize when using the word *cousin* as a substitute for Ruth's name.

    "Hey, Cousin, it's been a long time since I've seen you."

Let's try some more.

   Don't capitalize: "Tomorrow my aunt is coming to get me."

- **Do capitalize:** "Tomorrow my Aunt Sheila is coming to get me."
- **Do capitalize:** "What took you so long, Aunt?"

   Don't capitalize: "I got this gift for my uncle's birthday."

- **Do capitalize:** "I think Uncle Bob will like this."
- **Do capitalize:** "Happy Birthday, Uncle!"

   Don't capitalize: "Come over and meet my grandma and grandpa."

- **Do capitalize:** "This is my Grandmother Evelyn and my Grandfather Howard."
- **Do capitalize:** "Grandma and Grandpa, when are you coming over?"

So here is the rule:

Capitalize only when the word is used as a title (*clue:* it is usually followed by the name) **or when it is used as a substitute for a name** (*clue:* try using the name instead to see if it fits.) For example, you would not say "I got this gift for my Bob," instead of "I got this gift for my uncle." But you would say "Happy Birthday, Bob!" instead of "Happy Birthday, Uncle Bob!"

Do you think you have it figured out? Try the exercise on the next page to see how you do.

Capitalization

It's All Relative *(cont.)*

In the following sentences, circle the letters that need to be changed to capitals and write the capital letters above. If there is a capitalized word that should *not* be capitalized, draw a line through the appropriate letter.

1. uncle Jorge sat on the front porch.
2. I said, "mom, what I really want to do is stay home!"
3. My mom and my dad won't be home until 7 P.M.
4. His grandma made a quilt for his birthday.
5. My Cousin and my Grandma will be coming with my mom.
6. Our Grandparents have a surprise for Aunt Aimee.
7. "Dear grandma," I wrote at the top of my stationery.
8. I wish my aunt lived closer to us; she looks just like mom.
9. Then dad stopped and looked behind him.
10. I like to go to grandmother Norton's house in the summer.
11. My favorite Cousin is Jimmy because he makes me laugh.
12. At the wedding we saw aunt Marsha and cousin Brad.
13. My Mom and Dad are taking me to dinner after the awards assembly.
14. At the reunion I saw Aunt Edith and uncle Jacques, and Cousins Kathy, Meredith, Hector, and Samantha.
15. For my birthday I'm inviting cousin Sarah, Cousin Leigh, aunt Susie, and my uncle, whose name is Mike.

Extension: Make a family chart on a large piece of butcher paper. Put your name and a picture of yourself (a photograph or a self-drawn portrait) in the proper position. If you have brothers and/or sisters, put their names (and pictures if you wish) next to yours. Your parents' names should appear above yours. Make as many lines as you need to represent your grandparents, aunts, uncles, and cousins. Be sure the lines appear in logical positions. A sample diagram appears below.

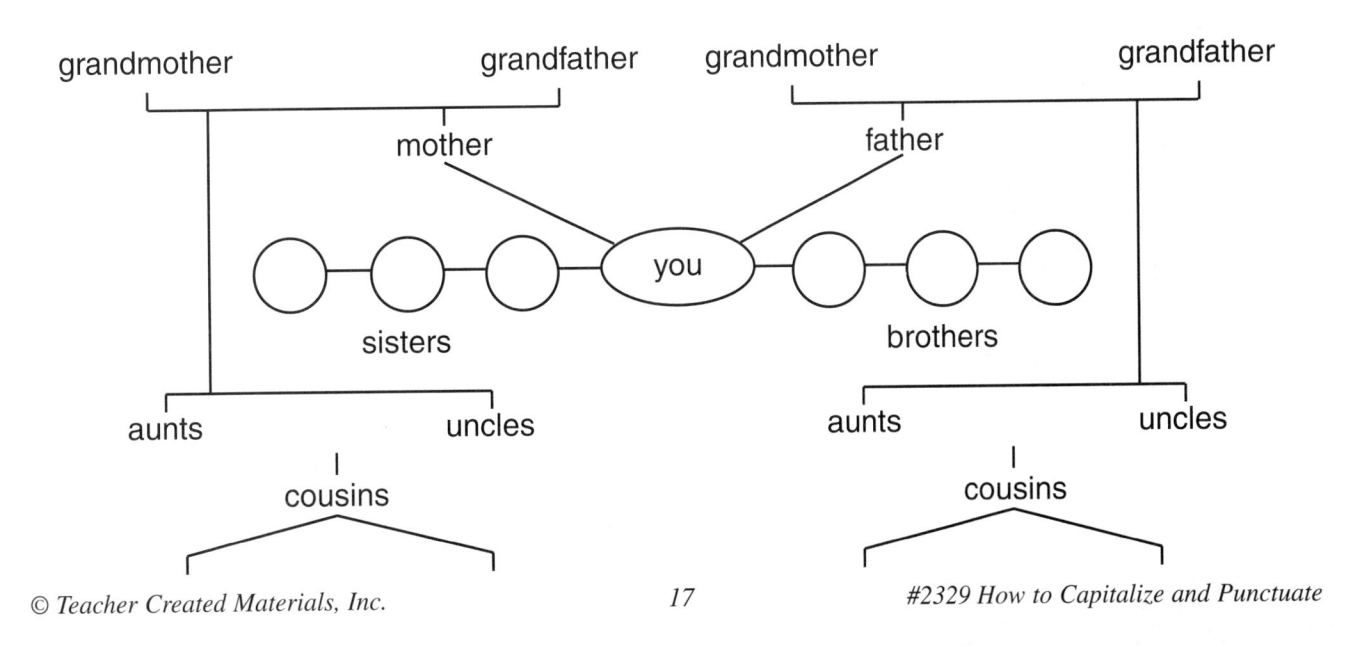

Capitalization

Subjects, Organizations, and Everything Else

What is your favorite subject in school? _____

If you wrote "Spanish," did you capitalize it? If so, you followed the correct capitalization rule. If you wrote "science," did you leave it uncapitalized? If so, you were right again.

- **All languages are always capitalized.** That's easy to remember. But here is where it gets complicated. School subjects are *sometimes* capitalized and *sometimes not*. Here is how you tell the difference.
- **If it is a general subject** like *science, math, history, social studies, art*, etc., you **do not capitalize**.
- **If it is a specific course** with a specific name, you **do capitalize.**
  A specific course name would be one that has a title like *Family Living, American Artists, Heroes and Myths*, etc.
- **The names of companies and organizations** are also capitalized.

  • General Motors   • Woodbridge High School   • Parent-Teacher

  On the line after each of these uncapitalized subjects, companies, and organizations, write them with the correct capitalization. (Some may not need a change.)

  1. shell oil company _____
  2. latin _____
  3. algebra _____
  4. first national bank _____
  5. oak grove elementary school _____
  6. european modern art _____
  7. miller publishing house _____
  8. world tennis association _____
  9. science _____
  10. english _____

- There are a few more things that are always capitalized. They are the names of *races, nationalities*, and *religions*. Here are some examples.

Races:	Nationalities:	Religions:
African American	Russian	Buddhism
Caucasian	Japanese	Judaism
Asian	Irish	Taoism
Hispanic	Italian	Christianity

#2329 How to Capitalize and Punctuate

Capitalization

Capital Art

Have you ever thought of letters as art? They are an art form. In the days before computers, artists would hand-letter advertisements. It was a careful and meticulous art form that required special skills. Today there are people who do *calligraphy*, a form of artistic lettering. This also requires special skill. You don't need to be a commercial artist or a calligrapher to enjoy letters as art. You can take the capital letters of your choice, maybe your initials, and see what you can do with them. Here are some ways:

- Perhaps the simplest thing you could do with your letters would be to write them next to each other and then see what kind of art you could form from the arrangement.

- In medieval times, scholars created what was known as *illuminated manuscripts* where special letters were highly decorated. We don't often use such an ornate style today, but you can try something like the letter *F* shown here. Do you see why it might start the words for *Fourth of July*?

- Sometimes it's fun to form letters out of drawings of people bending, jumping, and joining hands. Or animals might make interesting letters:

- You can also create doodle art using words or stringing the alphabet on a page:

Extension: Using a friend's name or a word like "Mommy" or "Grandpa," create art and frame it as a gift.

Capitalization

Capital Art *(cont.)*

Here are some letters that are waiting for a makeover. Can you turn them into a picture with your doodles?

V
W   F
G   A
S   O
K
U   Z
L   X
R

#2329 How to Capitalize and Punctuate © Teacher Created Materials, Inc.

Capitalization

Review

It is time to see how much you have learned about capitalization. Circle all the letters below that should be capitals. (*Hint:* there are 63 of them.)

1. the first day of school is exciting.

2. freddy wilson's frog peepers hopped into mrs. woolsey's purse.

3. as i walked outside, i smelled smoke.

4. In the play, robin hood was played by lieutenant bronksy.

5. the fourth thursday in november is thanksgiving.

6. i like halloween best when it is on a saturday.

7. aunt susan went to yellowstone national park.

8. connie lives on maple street in bismark, north dakota.

9. brazil, argentina, and peru are in south america.

10. the mediterranean sea and the atlantic ocean touch spain.

11. the letter was signed, "love always, esther."

12. davis medical center opened in january last year.

13. one of the religions practiced by many african people is islam.

14. italians and germans belong to the caucasian race.

15. last tuesday ruben walked his dog spotty down tulip street to central park.

Capitalization

Capital Game

Here is a game to play with capitalization. Make three copies of page 23 for each person. (If you need more vowels, more copies can be made.) Glue these alphabet pages to a piece of cardboard and cut out the letters. Put your name or initials on the backs of your letter cards so you can identify your set of cards after games with many players. Your teacher may be able to laminate your letters so they will last longer. You can play this two ways:

Solo

1. Mix up the cards and place them in a stack facedown. Put a piece of paper and pencil nearby.

2. Draw five cards and set a timer for 10 minutes.

3. Look at your cards and see if you can make a word from the letters in your hand. If you can, spread it out in front of you and draw five more cards.

4. If you cannot, draw one other card and make a mark on your paper. Each time you need to draw another card, make another mark on your paper.

5. Play for 10 minutes if you can. When the timer goes off, stop.

6. Look at all the words in front of you. If you can make a sentence out of any of them, give yourself minus five points for each sentence. If you can make one complete sentence using all your words, give yourself minus 20 points.

7. Look carefully at all the words and sentences (if any) that you have made. Make a mark on your paper for every time there is a word that is not capitalized when it should be. Also, make a mark for every time a word is capitalized when it should not be.

8. Count how many marks are on your paper and subtract any minus points you earned. The object is to have as few points as possible. Keep track of your scores to see if you do better each time.

With Others

To play this game with up to six other people, mix all your cards together and place them facedown in the center of the table. Write your names at the top of a piece of paper and have someone keep score. Deal out five cards to each player to begin the game. Put a mark under each player's name for each time he or she needs to draw another card. Each player builds words on the table at his or her place. You may set a timer if you only play for a set amount of time. When the timer goes off, the one with the lowest score wins. If you have more time, you can play until you run out of cards.

Extension: Try a Capital Game tournament with the winners playing the other winners. Try playing the game like Scrabble, with your words being added to the words of other players.

Capitalization

Capital Game (cont.)

A	B	C	D	E	F
G	H	I	J	K	L
M	N	O	P	Q	R
S	T	U	V	W	X
Y	Z	a	b	c	d
e	f	g	h	i	j
k	l	m	n	o	p
q	r	s	t	u	v
w	x	y	z	E	e

Punctuation

When and Why to Punctuate

IMAGINEREADINGASTORYTHATHASNOPUNCTUATIONANDNOSPACESSOEVERYTHINGRUNSTOGEHTHERHOWDIFFICULTWOULDITBETOCOMMUNICATEWITHOTHERSDONTYOUTHINKTHATWOULDBEAMESSYOURERIGHTITWOULDBEAMESSPEOPLEWOULDHAVESOMUCHTROUBLEBEINGUNDERSTOODWOULDNTTHEYPUNCTUATIONWASINVENTEDTOBEANIMPORTANTPARTOFOURLANGUAGESYSTEMPUNCTUATIONMARKSMAKEITPOSSIBLEFORUSTOMANAGEOURWORDSANDIDEASANDTHEYHELPTHEREADERUNDERSTANDJUSTEXACTLYWHATITISTHATYOUWANTTOSAY.

Did you manage to read what is written above? If you did, was it very difficult? (If you couldn't read it at all, there is a "translation" in the answer key). Punctuation marks are like markers on the highway—they tell us which way to go, when to slow down and when to stop.

The Basics of Punctuation

Apostrophes
- **Use apostrophes for contractions.**
  You've got to come and visit soon. I'm missing you!
- **Use apostrophes to show possession or ownership with nouns.**
  Amber's dad found David's wallet in the Fletchers' car.
- **Use apostrophes also to show the plurals of letters and words but *not* for other plurals.**
  Erin got three *A's* on her report card.
  Jake used too many *very's* in his story.
  Erin has three kittens in a basket.
  Jake shot three baskets at the game last night.

Colons
- **Use a colon in a business letter right after the greeting.**
  Dear Sirs: Dear Mrs. Gonzales:
- **Use a colon to introduce a list.**
  Please bring the following items to school: white paper, colored pencils, and a compass.
- **Use a colon between the hour and the minutes of the time of day.**
  5:30 A.M. 3:15 P.M.
- **Use a colon to introduce a long, direct quotation.**

At the Galaxy Alien Convention, the keynote speaker said:

> *Things are looking up for space aliens these days. We can now make Earthlings better looking! Our handsome bug eyes, snake-like tongues, and slimy ears are easily cloned to replace ugly human features. Not only can we can help the poor things raise their self-esteem, but we will finally be able to view them without throwing up!*

(*Hint:* There are no quotation marks around the passage above. If you wonder why, it is because you don't use them with a long, direct quote. Instead, indent on both sides to set it off from the other text).

#2329 How to Capitalize and Punctuate

Punctuation

When and Why to Punctuate *(cont.)*

Commas

- **Use a comma between two independent clauses joined by *or*, *and*, or *but*.**

  There are always creative excuses for not turning in homework, but no excuse is acceptable.

  My dad loves music, and my mom loves to sing.

- **Use a comma after a dependent clause that comes at the beginning of a sentence.**

  Even though I forgot my notes, I still did a good job on my speech.

- **Use a comma between words, phrases, or clauses that are a series of three or more things.**

  I will be writing a report that is brilliant, insightful, and a delight to read.

  My mother asked me to feed the dog, take out the trash, and fold all my baby brother's diapers.

  My brothers are Jason (who is scientific), Michael (who is artistic), and Chris (who is musical).

- **Use commas to set apart hundreds, thousands, and millions, etc., when writing numbers.**

  My brother had 234,556,000 telephone messages when we got home, and they were all from girls!

- **Use a comma to set apart the city from a state and a street from a city.**

  When I grow up I intend to live at 12234 Monster Mash Lane, Transylvania, PA.

- **Use a comma between the day and the year in a date.**

  June 17, 1983

- **Use a comma after a greeting or a closing in a letter to a friend or relative.**

  Dear Granny,

  Lovingly yours,

- **Use a comma after introductory words at the beginning of a sentence or after an interjection (an introductory exclamation).**

  Yes, of course you may dye your hair purple.

  No kidding, I dyed my hair purple.

- **Use a comma after an interjection that is not an exclamation.**

  Oh, I don't know what I'll do.

- **Use a comma to separate the person to whom you are speaking from the rest of the sentence.**

  Julie, I heard you dyed your hair purple.

- **Use a comma to set off dialogue.**

  Her mom asked, "What on earth happened to your hair?"

  She said, "You don't remember?" and she walked into the light so her mom could get a better look. "You told me it was okay to dye it purple."

- **Use commas to set off interruptions.**

  My dog will do the craziest things. The other day, for example, he was eating broccoli.

© Teacher Created Materials, Inc. 25 #2329 *How to Capitalize and Punctuate*

Punctuation

When and Why to Punctuate (cont.)

- **Use commas to set off appositives** (words or phrases that explain, identify, or rename a noun or pronoun).
  Licorice, my dog, tore a hole in the screen to get a tortilla!
  My sister, the world's smartest girl, forgot her orthodontist appointment.
- **Use commas to set off phrases.**
  Positive-negative film, rarely used except in the movie industry and by some photographers, will take negatives, prints, and slides.
  A drooling, snarling dog chased me across the park, over a fence, and into a trash bin.
- **Use commas between two adjectives that modify the same noun.**
  We drove all day across the dry, dusty desert.

Dashes

- **Use a dash to indicate a sudden break in a sentence.**
  There is one thing that really bugs me about my brother—no, actually there are a zillion things—but it really bugs me when my friends call and he puts them on hold and forgets all about them.
- **Use a dash to add emphasis to a word, a series of words, a phrase, or a clause.**
  Let me just remind you that you will need to complete all the requirements—have a title page, a bibliography, and a video—in order to get the highest possible grade.
- **Use a dash to show that someone's speech is being interrupted.**
  Hello—yes, I remembered—what?—oh, okay—no, that really won't be necessary—no, really—I mean it—no, of course not—really, you don't need to—I really mean it, you don't need to—don't.

Ellipses

- **An ellipsis is three spaced periods used to replace words that have been left out or to indicate a pause in dialogue.**
  . . . ah . . . well . . . it's like this . . . ah . . . aliens came down . . . that's it . . . they came down in this huge saucer and sucked up my homework with some strange vacuum-like device!
  Twinkle, twinkle . . . like a diamond in the sky.
- **When an ellipsis ends a sentence, add a period, making it a total of four dots.**
  I was thinking of going with you, but . . . .

Exclamation Points

- **An exclamation mark is used to show strong feeling after a word, a phrase or an exclamatory sentence.** (Be careful with exclamation points; they should not be overused. And don't ever use multiple exclamation marks all in a row!!!)
  Oh no! My underwear just fell out the window!

Hyphens

- **Use a hyphen to break a word between syllables at the end of a line.**
  I don't like that movie because it is too much like a car-
  toon.

When and Why to Punctuate (cont.)

Note: Avoid dividing words with five letters or less, don't ever try to divide one-syllable words, and don't divide contractions or abbreviations.

- **Use a hyphen with two-part numbers.**
  forty-eight   twenty-three
- **Use hyphens when writing fractions as words.**
  one-fourth   four-tenths
- **Use hyphens to create new words.**
  We found some fat-free chips.
  You've got an I-know-something-you-don't-know look on your face.
- **Use hyphens for compound nouns and adjectives.**
  drive-through bank   four-year-old boy
  G-rated   e-mail

Parentheses

- **Use parentheses around words or phrases that add information or make an idea more clear.**
  For more information about llama toenails, read chapter 13 (pages 56–72).
  The national park had something for everyone, including the fit (trails, mountain climbing, and whitewater rafting), the consumer (shops and concession stands), the curious (nature centers, museums, and ranger tours), and the tired (hammocks, benches, and cabins).
  He asked his neighbor Paul (he's a whiz with cars) to help him repair his truck.
- **Use parentheses around an abbreviation after you have written the full name.**
  My high school is on the same street as Jet Propulsion Lab (JPL).

Periods

- **Use a period at the end of a declarative or imperative sentence that is not an exclamation.**
  Always turn off the light when you leave the room.
  My puppy chewed my algebra book.
  In the future most of us will be telecommuting.
- **Use periods after initials.**
  A. A. Milne   Mr. P. J. Winterhouse
- **Use periods after abbreviations.**
  P.O. Box 987
  234 Slippery Hill St.
  Mt. Awesome, CA

Question Marks

- **Use a question mark at the end of an interrogative sentence** (a question) **and to show doubt about the accuracy of a figure or fact.**
  What were you thinking when you decided to do that?
  By the year 2040 (?) marine biologists will be living in laboratories on the ocean floor.

Punctuation

When and Why to Punctuate *(cont.)*

Quotation Marks

- **Use quotation marks to set off the words of a direct quote.**
  I was laughing so hard. When my brother woke up this morning, he came out of his room all rumpled and said, "I don't know what President Lincoln would do because I haven't asked him."

- **Use quotation marks to indicate the title of an article in a magazine or newspaper.**
  I cut out an article titled "My Best Friend, Llama" from yesterday's paper.

- **Use quotation marks to indicate the title of a chapter.**
  Read the chapter titled "My Brother, the Denizen of the Deep."

- **Use quotation marks to indicate the titles of essays and short stories.**
  My essay, "How I Almost Spent My Summer Vacation," was in the school newspaper.
  My mom just sold a short story titled "Jackie, the Mad Hugger."

- **Use quotation marks to indicate the titles of songs and poems.**
  My dad keeps listening to "Free as a Bird" on the CD player. It's starting to drive me crazy!
  I am going to read "Bed in Summer" by Robert Louis Stevenson.

- **Use quotation marks around certain words used in a special way.**
  I can't believe I got "punctuation" right on the spelling test!
  Please send me your e-mail address or I will have to send this by "snail mail."
  I called my brother a "dork" after he called me a "dweeb."

- **A quote within a quote uses only one quotation mark at each end of the inside quote.**
  She said, "He told me that 'The Little Princess' is his favorite poem."
  "Listen," Amber said, "Mr. Zone clearly stated, 'Do not leave CDs in the CD-ROM drive!'"

Semicolons

- (A semicolon is like a cross between a period and a comma.) **Use a semicolon to join the independent clauses of a compound sentence when you are not using a comma and a conjunction.**
  My mom got a scanner for the computer; I couldn't wait to try it.

- **Use a semicolon in front of a conjunction when you are joining two simple sentences.**
  She usually adores frozen yogurt; however, today she didn't want any.

- **Use a semicolon in a series of three or more items when commas are used within those items.**
  Our talent show has been planned. We will have Jazz, a group of dancers; Klutzy Kyle, a magical extravaganza; Barknikov, a poodle ballet dancer; and Spring Showers, a folk singer.

Punctuation

End Marks

Every sentence ends with a punctuation mark. Some sentences are "telling" sentences (a declarative sentence which makes a statement), and these end with periods. Other sentences are "asking" sentences (an interrogative sentence which asks a question), and these end with question marks. Another kind of sentence is a "commanding" sentence (an imperative sentence which makes a request), which also ends with a period. And then, last but not least, there are sentences which show strong feelings or surprise (an exclamatory sentence which makes an exclamation), which end with an exclamation mark.

Here is an example of each kind.

Declarative Sentence

An insect is sometimes called a bug.

Interrogative Sentence

Do you know anything about insects?

Imperative Sentence

Close the lid to the bug box.

Exclamatory Sentence

Oh no, the bugs are escaping!

Here is a chart to remind you of what kind of punctuation to use.

.	Declarative Sentence
?	Interrogative Sentence
.	Imperative Sentence
!	Exclamatory Sentence

© Teacher Created Materials, Inc.   29   #2329 *How to Capitalize and Punctuate*

Punctuation

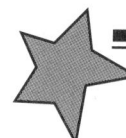

End Marks (cont.)

Put a period, a question mark, or an exclamation mark at the end of each sentence below, and on the line after the sentence, write "*declarative*," "*interrogative*," "*imperative*," or "*exclamatory*."

1. Oh boy, it's time for recess _____

2. I'm not sure where to go because I'm new here _____

3. Where do I go for recess _____

4. Do you mean "way over there where it's all sandy" _____

5. Oh well, at least there are some swings over here _____

6. Hey, watch where you're going _____

7. Don't throw sand _____

8. Now that's an interesting looking ball _____

9. Where did you get it _____

10. Be careful where you throw that thing _____

11. Can I play too _____

12. I'm not kidding, I really like to play _____

13. Oh no, there goes the bell _____

14. Okay class, let's line up _____

15. I really didn't get much of a chance to play, but I suppose I already had my chance when I was little; now I need to be the teacher _____

Punctuation

Abbreviations

An abbreviation is a shortened form of a word that is usually followed by a period. An abbreviation is never used by itself as a word. It is always used with other words or names.

- You **wouldn't** write . . .

  I live on the St. next to the park.

- You **would** write . . .

  I live at 4342 Pumpkin St. next to the park.

- And you **wouldn't** write . . .

  That's a Mt. I would like to climb.

- But you **would** write . . .

  Someday I want to climb Mt. Whitney.

Here are some common abbreviations:

apt.	apartment	cont.	continued	Jr.	Junior
Aug.	August	Corp.	Corporation	kg	kilogram
Ave.	Avenue	Dec.	December	lb.	pound
Bldg.	Building	Dept.	Department	Oct.	October
Blvd.	Boulevard	ft.	feet	oz.	ounces
Capt.	Captain	in.	inches	Rd.	Road
cm	centimeters	Jan.	January		

Match the abbreviations with the words they stand for. Then, please copy the abbreviation correctly. Don't forget periods!

Letter **Abbreviation**

_____ 1. Wed.   a. Boulevard _____
_____ 2. Mr.   b. Mister _____
_____ 3. St.   c. year _____
_____ 4. Dec.   d. Governor _____
_____ 5. U.S.   e. December _____
_____ 6. Capt.   f. tablespoon _____
_____ 7. Tbs.   g. Tuesday _____
_____ 8. Blvd.   h. Street _____
_____ 9. Aug.   i. gallon _____
_____ 10. Gov.   j. Captain _____
_____ 11. jr.   k. Doctor _____
_____ 12. gal.   l. United States _____
_____ 13. Dr.   m. junior _____
_____ 14. Tues.   n. Wednesday _____
_____ 15. yr.   o. August _____

© Teacher Created Materials, Inc.   31   #2329 How to Capitalize and Punctuate

Punctuation

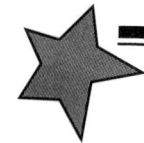

Contractions

A *contraction* is one word that you squeeze together (contract) from two words. Contractions are useful in conversation and letters to friends. In formal writing such as research reports and serious essays, limit the number of contractions you use. To make a contraction, leave out one or more letters from the original two words and replace them with an apostrophe. Here are some common contractions:

I'm	I am	that'll	that will
I'll	I will	that's	that is, that has
I've	I have	let's	let us
you'll	you will	aren't	are not
you're	you are	can't	cannot
he's	he is, he has	didn't	did not
she'll	she will	wouldn't	would not
it's	it is, it has	weren't	were not
we've	we have	won't	will not
we're	we are	there's	there is
they've	they have	there've	there have
they're	they are	must've	must have
who's	who is, who has	must'nt	must not

Be careful of these most common contraction errors.

❏ **it's** and **its**

It's is the contraction for *it is*. *Its* is the possessive form of *it*.
People are used to using an apostrophe to indicate a possessive with nouns such as, *That is Sarah's bicycle*. But remember, you don't always have to use an apostrophe to indicate possession: *That is her bicycle*. Here is a sentence to help you see the difference.
It's always noisy when a peacock spreads its feathers and makes its morning call.

❏ **their, there,** and **they're**

Their is a possessive pronoun.
 Their dog is really hairy.
There is an adverb used to indicate a location.
 Leave that porcupine there.
They're is the contraction for *they are*.
 They told me that they're not coming.

❏ **your, you're**

Your is a possessive pronoun.
 Please pick up your clothes.
You're is the contraction for *you are*.
 You're invited to a surprise party.

Contractions (cont.)

Here is your opportunity to make contractions. In the story below, underline any words that may be combined into a contraction. On another paper list the contractions. There are 52.

✧ ✧ ✧

I cannot believe it. I wrote 25 invitations that said: "You are invited to a surprise party for Serena. Do not tell her or she will not come." We could not have the party on any day but the 18th because it is close to Serena's birthday, and it is the only day in the entire month of April that is free. I stamped them and said to my dog, Sugar, "Let us mail these before it is too late." You will not believe what happened next.

It must have taken Sugar and me three hours just to mail the invitations after I had spent six hours making them because Sugar must have stopped at every tree. And then she barked at every bird; she would lie down if I tried to hurry her. Then she chased a cat up a tree, and she did not want to leave. There have been some new families who have moved in down the street, so Sugar wanted to sniff each of their new driveways. There must have been a dozen. A huge dog came running out at us. I should not have run, but I could not help it. It is instinctive to run when a snarling dog appears. It would have eaten us both alive, or at least that is what I was thinking when I decided that I had better run. I ran, dragging Sugar at the same time because she had decided that she would save the universe from the world's meanest dog. I will make a long story short by telling you that while I was trying to avoid death and while Sugar was trying to save the universe, the mean dog would have had us both for breakfast, but all three of us ended up tangled together in a whimpering, snarling knot of fur and tasty human skin. I was not doing a very good job of getting out of the mess, but at least the dogs were also stuck so we were not going anywhere. Then I heard a voice, "Who is this, Fluffy? It looks like we are meeting our neighbors." Fluffy? I was thinking it would have been better to name this dog Terminator. There I was. I was covered with dog slobber and fur, and I was not a pretty sight. Instead of meeting a new neighbor while standing, I could not believe that I was saying hello on my back while one dog, which should not be allowed on the street, was sitting on my stomach and drooling on my face, and another dog, which would not ever be allowed out of the house again, was licking my leg. What is wrong with this picture? My very good-looking neighbor must not have a very interesting life because he was laughing and enjoying the whole thing.

And if that were not enough, when I got home my mother told me that she would have stopped me if she had known that I was mailing the invitations. I had not been gone for three minutes when my sister called and told my mom that she had decided when to have her wedding and that she would like me to be a bridesmaid. Here is the part that convinces me that it is not a good idea to get out of bed on some days. She has decided to have her wedding on the 18th—you know, the day of Serena's surprise party? She has already reserved the church. I am so embarrassed. Now I will need to cancel the party. And my neighbor still laughs at me every time he sees me.

Punctuation

That's Mine!

When a word shows that something belongs to it, it shows ownership. *Possession* is another word for ownership. An apostrophe is used to show possession.

Example: *Friskie's leash* (To whom does the leash belong? The leash belongs to the dog, Friskie.) You usually add *'s* to a word to show possession. Show possession in the following examples. Don't forget the apostrophe. The first two have been completed for you.

1. food belonging to a cat — the cat's food
2. a nest belonging to a bird — a bird's nest
3. a bike belonging to Miguel _____
4. a store that is owned by Kim _____
5. a CD player belonging to David _____
6. a book belonging to my sister _____
7. a skateboard owned by my brother _____
8. some toys that belong to a baby _____
9. a desk that belongs to the teacher _____
10. a brush that belongs to a painter _____

✧ ✧ ✧

Rewrite each sentence below, adding an apostrophe where one is needed to show possession.

1. Nicky ran screaming into Manuels house.

2. My dad knocked down a hornets nest.

3. I wish I could drive my brothers car.

4. An alien ate Marielas homework.

5. Grandpas spaghetti is the best in the world.

Punctuation

When and Where?

A comma is used when writing a date. The comma separates the date and the year. It is also used to separate the day and the date.
- October 21, 1980
- Friday, September 23

Insert commas where needed in the sentences below.
1. My parents bought their first home on January 13 1976.
2. My mom was born on March 31 1948.
3. We went to Disneyland on Tuesday August 18 and it was really crowded!
4. My brother's birthday is November 17 1973.
5. On Saturday April 19, we are flying to my grandma's house.
6. I get my tonsils out on Monday September 16 and then I can eat lots of ice cream.
7. Our puppies were born on February 14 1997.
8. It rained cats and dogs on January 18 1995.
9. Aliens reprogrammed my little brother on Wednesday June 17.
10. I will be a wart hog on Friday October 31.

Write these dates using commas correctly.
1. today's date and year _____
2. today's day and date _____
3. your birthday _____
4. your favorite day of the year (besides your birthday) _____
5. the birthdate of a member of your family (and tell who) _____

Use a comma between the city and state (or province) in an address.
- Los Angeles, California (city, state)

Add commas to the following sentences.
1. Yesterday, I met a girl from Canberra Australia.
2. A hurricane went to shore at Acapulco Mexico.
3. I've never been to Seattle Washington.
4. It can get very cold in Buffalo New York.
5. Yesterday, I received e-mail from Bordeaux France.
6. Many movie stars live in La Canada-Flintridge California.
7. Alexandria Virginia, is an interesting historic town.
8. You can take a great train ride in Durango Colorado.
9. Have you been on the roller coasters in St. Louis Missouri?
10. The mountains are really high in Vail Colorado.

Answer the following with the name of a city and state or province.
1. Where were you born? _____
2. Where was your mother born? _____
3. Where do you live today? _____
4. Name where one of your grandparents lives. _____
5. Where is the last place you visited? _____

© Teacher Created Materials, Inc. #2329 *How to Capitalize and Punctuate*

Punctuation

Where's My List?

A comma is used between words in a series. Three or more things together make a series.

We will be talking today about muffins, kittens, and lollipops.

Add the missing commas to the sentences below.

1. All birds have feathers wings and beaks.
2. My sister is sleepy grumpy and clueless.
3. I would have done my homework but I was abducted by aliens was left in Siberia and had to wait for the Marines to rescue me.
4. I ordered a pizza with cheese pickles and sliced cherries.
5. Please go to the store and get flypaper chopsticks and kumquats.
6. I went to the door with rollers in my hair a mud mask on my face and wearing my headgear.
7. My dog has brown spots a short tail and fuzzy feet.
8. My little brother can't go anywhere without his blanket his stuffed duck and his rabbit's foot key chain.
9. When I go to college, I am taking a stereo a microwave and a treadmill.
10. For her birthday, Mindy wants some edible flowers sparkly socks and a pony.

✧   ✧   ✧

A comma is also used between two or more describing words (adjectives).

A friendly, playful dog makes a good pet.

Add the missing commas to the sentences below.

1. My rabbit has long floppy ears.
2. A large heavy sparrow could weigh 200 pounds.
3. My teacher has a green pointy nose.
4. My dad used to have curly frizzy hair.
5. A friendly playful giraffe ate all my spaghetti.

#2329 How to Capitalize and Punctuate

Punctuation

Set It Off!

If a comma were a road sign, it would be yellow and it would say, "pause." Commas are very useful for telling readers when to slow down.

Here are some ways to use commas for this purpose.

- ❏ **Use a comma after the words *yes, no, well*, and *all right*.** They should also be used after phrases like "No kidding," and "Of course." These kinds of words and phrases are called *interjections,* and they are separated from the rest of the sentence with a comma.
  - Yes, I did stay up all night at the slumber party.
  - No, we didn't go to Marc's house.
  - Well, it's a long story.
  - All right, we were going to Marc's house but he wasn't home.
  - No kidding, you know where he was?
  - Of course, but I won't tell anyone.

- ❏ **When a person is being addressed, a comma is used to separate his or her name from the rest of the sentence.**
  - Jeremy Jackson, get in here right this minute!
  - Erin, would you like some help with that banana split you are trying to eat?
  - Don't worry, Jaime, we'll find your boa constrictor.

- ❏ **Use commas to set off interruptions when a word, phrase, or clause interrupts the main thought of a sentence.** To check that a word, phrase, or clause is an interruption, see if that part of the sentence can be removed without changing the meaning of the sentence, or see if the interruption can be placed nearly anywhere in the sentence without changing its meaning.
  - Most dogs think that the humans they live with are part of their doggy family. Our dog, for example, likes to eat her dog food whenever my daughter appears.
  You can remove "for example," and the sentence will still make sense. You can also move the phrase.
  - For example, our dog likes to eat her dog food whenever my daughter appears.
  - Our dog likes to eat her dog food, for example, whenever my daughter appears.

- ❏ **Use commas to set off an appositive** (an explanatory word or phrase) **from the rest of the sentence.**
  - Mr. Gargoyle, my science teacher, says he is going to visit all of his students on Halloween.
  - My best friend, Lucy Licorice, lives on a houseboat.

- ❏ **Also use commas to set off phrases and clauses.**
  - In bookstores of the future, we will find books stored on disks instead of on shelves.
  - English, which students learn throughout the world, is the most widely used language in all fields of medicine and science.

Punctuation

Set It Off! *(cont.)*

In the sentences below, add the missing commas to "set it off."

1. No Marlene does not like being squirted in the face.

2. Christopher how long have you been on the telephone?

3. Well just what did you have in mind?

4. Sure Laura I'd love another jelly donut.

5. My brother the world's scariest boy likes escargots.

6. The plane we are taking a 747 will have plenty of room.

7. You realize of course that you will not be allowed out of the house in that outfit.

8. My orthodontist Dr. Baugh decorated his office for Halloween.

9. All right if that's what you think, let's just eat all of the chocolate.

10. In the future we will be able to speak to our computers.

11. No kidding you went rock climbing?

12. We went to Bouquet Canyon a canyon near Valencia to attend a harvest festival.

13. You could read for example some books about the historical period in which your novel takes place.

14. For Valentine's Day my dad gave me two pounds of my favorite treat candy corn.

15. I don't care what you think I'm going to go back there and help that little boy.

Punctuation

May I Quote You?

- ❏ **Quotation marks are those little marks that are used at the beginning and end of the exact words that someone speaks or has written.**
  A *quotation* is what you call the exact words. A quotation is either the words someone speaks in dialogue or conversation or the words that a writer has written and that you are borrowing.
  - "Hello," Maria said.
  - "Hi, how are you?" Luis replied.
  - And then my mom said, "I assume that you have finished your homework."
  - In the book *Travels in Time*, author Rex T. All says, "Time is relative. One need not be an Einstein to understand this concept." And then the author presents some experiments that anyone can try at home.

- ❏ **Use quotation marks for the titles of songs, poems, short stories, articles, chapters of books, and television and radio programs.**
  - On television's "Monday Night Football," she sang "The Star-Spangled Banner."
  - Have you read Jack London's short story "To Build a Fire"?

- ❏ **Also, you may use quotation marks to indicate a special word.**
  A special word might be a word which is being discussed.
  - Do you know when to use the words "there" and "their"?
  - "Up" has different meanings—for example, "He looked up the word" and "He looked up the drainpipe."

  A special word (or words) might be slang.
  - He says he wants to be a "nerd."
  - She is always telling her sister to "chill out."

- ❏ **Or quotation marks might be used to show that a word or a phrase is being used in a special way.**
  - When my mom escorts my little brother on Halloween, she says she is being a "fright attendant."

- ❏ **If you find yourself with a quote inside a quote, there is a special way of punctuating**.
  You use the single quote mark for the inside quote.
  - Jackie said, "My teacher is so mean. I told her I needed an extra day to finish my assignment because I got sick. She said, 'If you're well enough to come to school, you're well enough to do your homework.' I guess she would prefer for me to stay home after I am feeling better."

Punctuation

May I Quote You? *(cont.)*

In the sentences below, place a check mark in front of those that need their quotation marks to be corrected. On the line after each sentence, write the sentence again with the correct punctuation. If the sentence is correctly punctuated, write what kind of quotation you read: *exact words*, *title*, *a special word*, or *a quote within a quote*. The first two have been completed for you.

1. What is that bizarre thing upon your head? It looks like an octopus, said Mr. Grimmy.
   "What is that bizarre thing upon your head? It looks like an octopus," said Mr. Grimmy.

2. The teacher told the students to read the story, "The Raven," by Friday.
   title

3. I call my sister Idget, but I have no idea why.

4. "Hey!" Jacques shouted, "Didn't you hear the coach? He said, 'Stop when you get to the fence!'"

5. And then I will cover you with fragrant rose petals, Mama said, and sing a lullaby.

6. I found a book that said, Dinosaurs may be more closely related to birds than to lizards.

7. We have family nicknames, and my brother's is "Greasy Bear."

8. Did you hear what Nicole said? Amy asked us. She said, You guys are just too chicken to try it. She doesn't know what she is talking about!

9. I thought you would be too cool to go on the merry-go-round with me.

10. She watched "Somewhere in Time" so many times she wore out the tape.

11. My brother always talks in his sleep. Last night he said, "Hurry and purple it before the snails get it!"

12. After we watched *Twister* we couldn't stop watching the clouds.

13. Come with us, Dad said, and we can stop for ice cream on the way.

14. I need to find the root word for transient.

15. Mom says we shouldn't say "Where's he at?" because it is not proper English.

#2329 How to Capitalize and Punctuate © Teacher Created Materials, Inc.

Punctuation

What Are These Funny Little Marks?

(Colons, Semicolons, and Hyphens)

❏ **Colons are used at the beginning of a list, after the greeting of a business letter, to introduce an important point, and between the numbers in time.** After each example below, create an example of your own on the back of this page.

- to introduce a list

  I am going to the beach and have packed the following items: a towel, sunscreen, water, a hat, swim fins, goggles, a surfboard, a beach ball, a book, and a cooler full of food.

  (*Hint*: Your list doesn't need to be so long. It just needs to be three or more items.)

- after the greeting in a business letter

  Dear Mr. Gottrocks:

- to introduce an important point

  And so, even though my sister and I fight every day, steal each other's clothes, and grump at each other at night, there is one thing that is always true, no matter what: we love each other.

- to indicate the time

  The time is 12:42 and fifteen seconds.

❏ **Semicolons are like a cross between a period and a comma.** They can be used somewhat like a period.

  My brother brought home a radio-controlled car; we couldn't wait to watch him use it.

- Also, semicolons can be used to separate clauses that are independent and long, have commas, or are separated by conjunctive adverbs. This sounds pretty complicated, but hang in there.

  Davey apologized for the monkey's behavior, which was really not acceptable, even to Davey; however, Mrs. Crabapple kept right on screaming and jumping up and down, which actually made her look more like a monkey than Davey's monkey ever did.

  Look in some old magazines or newspapers for sentences which use semicolons and find at least three examples to read aloud in class and discuss with your classmates.

❏ **Hyphens are used to divide words between syllables when you need to go to the next line.** They are used to join compound words. They are used between the numbers of fractions, to join letters and words, to create new words, and to avoid confusion or awkward spelling.

After each example of hyphens below, create your own example or find one in an old magazine and paste it on the back of this paper.

  If you were watching TV last night, you may have seen the last epi-
  sode of My Three Jungle Cats.
  I don't like dot-matrix printers.
  She is four-tenths of the way finished with that book.
  My mom needs to know if the movie is G-rated.
  I had to re-collect all the shells that got lost. (Not **recollect**).

© Teacher Created Materials, Inc.   41   #2329 How to Capitalize and Punctuate

Punctuation

Punctuate This!

Now that your students are more familiar with punctuation and how to use it, here are some activities you might want to try in class as a reward for all their hard work.

Sight

On large index cards or larger pieces of cardboard or poster board, place the images of punctuation marks, one to a card. You may do this by enlarging photocopied punctuation marks, hand drawing them with markers, or creating them in large sizes on the computer and then pasting the images to cardboard.

Let students take turns being responsible for the various punctuation marks while the class participates in story time together. Choose a story with lots of punctuation. Choose simpler stories in the beginning and progress to more difficult ones as your students get faster at punctuating. Go over each story one time to familiarize the students with the story and where it is punctuated. If your students need extra help in getting started, you may wish to put the story on a chart or the blackboard at first. As you read the story aloud and you come to the part where the punctuation appears, have the student with the appropriate punctuation pop up and hold up his or her sign. Go through the story at least twice in order to allow students the pleasure of anticipating their parts and acting quickly. This will also allow the students without punctuation marks to learn the story well enough to read it aloud with you. Be sure to allow each student an opportunity to punctuate.

Sound

When students become competent at this, or if they are more advanced, you can also assign a sound for each punctuation mark. Let students brainstorm sounds with you. A quick popping kind of sound would be good for a period. You might want a razzberry for a colon or dash, and maybe three tongue clicks for an ellipsis. Have students practice their sounds to be sure that they will remember them when story time comes. You may wish to use the sounds along with the signs. If your students have caught on quickly, you may prefer to use only the sounds. Read the story aloud to practice all the punctuation sounds, prompting the students. After enough practice, try the story a couple of times without prompting. Have students who need to make a sound pop up to make it. You may wish to add a motion to go with the sound—for instance, the student who makes the comma sound may make a swishing motion in the air as well.

Action

When you get really good at this, get your act together and take it on the road. Other students will be amazed and amused to watch this audio-kinetic demonstration of punctuation. You may also wish to perform for parents at an open house. The activity can be used all year long to help all students gain competency at punctuating with sound. A once-a-week session of Punctuate This! can be a reward at the end of a week of grammar lessons. Students can also bring in stories to be punctuated aloud.

Review

Here is a story that has no punctuation and no capitalization whatsoever. Your mission: capitalize and punctuate. Using a colored pen, write a capital letter over any letter that needs one. Be careful. Don't capitalize anything that shouldn't be. Insert punctuation marks wherever you think they need to go. Good luck!

◇　　　　　　　　◇　　　　　　　　◇

our class went on a very special field trip we saved up money from newspapers and recycling aluminum cans until we had enough for a group rate to disneyland isnt that exciting

we also had to save up enough for the bus which wasnt too expensive when the day finally came we were so excited we sang songs like bingo and the ants go marching in all the way there the bus driver said he was going to go crazy but he was just kidding because he was also going to disneyland and he was happy about that

when we got there marisa said i see space mountain then luke said I see the matterhorn mountain then hector said i see splash mountain and of course then olivia said i see thunder mountain

the bus driver said maybe they should call it mountainland instead nobody said anything because just then we all saw the monorail go by I want to go on the monorail cassie said but mrs martinez said that we had to go through the entrance first

after we went through the entrance everybody forgot about the monorail we were divided into groups so we could go wherever our group wanted to go and we could join with other groups too whenever we wanted to because we all wore bright orange shirts it wouldnt be too hard to find each other mrs martinez took a group and so did mr rawlings ms white mrs hojito and bill the bus driver guess what i was in bill the bus drivers group ill never forget this day our group had more fun than any other group because bill went on all the rides with us and he didnt complain at all in fact he said im having too much fun isnt that great bill the bus driver even rode the bobsleds with us and he went on the autopia too he didnt get sick on dumbo or the merry go round and he even went on splash mountain thunder mountain and space mountain on indiana jones he covered his eyes when a snake hissed at him and on the jungle cruise he shrieked when a hippopotamus blew water on him he made us all laugh all the time at the very end bill the bus driver got motion sickness on the teacups someone was coming to pick him up and to bring a new bus driver that meant we got to go back into disneyland for one more hour we felt sorry for bill but we were so glad to have another hour

Capitalization and Punctuation Posters

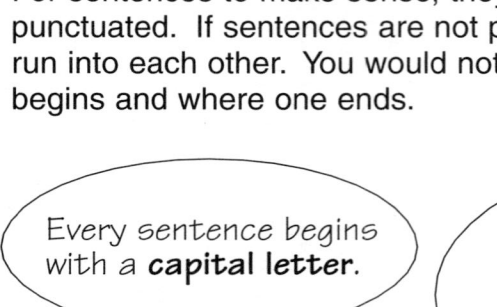

Comma Use

Use commas to separate words in a series.

Use a comma after the words *yes*, *no*, and *well* at the beginning of sentences.

Use a comma to set off a person's name when that person is being spoken to.

Pen, I am happy, proud, and excited to hear it.

Yes, I know all about commas, Pencil.

Capitalizing and Punctuating Sentences

For sentences to make sense, they must be punctuated. If sentences are not punctuated, they will run into each other. You would not know where one begins and where one ends.

*Every sentence ends with a **period**, a **question mark**, or an **exclamation point**.*

*Every sentence begins with a **capital letter**.*

#2329 How to Capitalize and Punctuate © Teacher Created Materials, Inc.

Capitalization and Punctuation Posters

More Comma Use

An **appositive** is a group of words that tells more about another word. Use two commas to set off an appositive from the rest of the sentence.

The **day** and the **year** in dates should be separated by commas.

The names of **cities** and **states** should be separated by commas.

Speech bubbles:
- "Was your mother planted in Springfield, Illinois?"
- "My mother, an oak tree, was just an acorn that fell to the ground on July 4, 1990."

Quotation Marks

Use quotation marks to show exactly what people are saying to each other.

A **direct quotation** is the **exact words spoken**. Quotation marks are used before and after a direct quotation, and commas are used to set off quotations.

When we write what a person says without showing exact words, we do not use quotation marks.

Speech bubbles:
- "My teacher says that pens are permanent."
- "Pencils are sharp," my teacher said.

© Teacher Created Materials, Inc. — #2329 How to Capitalize and Punctuate

Capitalization and Punctuation

Answer Key

Page 8 What's in a Name?
Pet Day at Wiggleworm Elementary School
Mrs. Wolfe was in charge, and she stood at the entrance of Wiggleworm Elementary School to welcome the students. Lindsay Harper entered first with her goldfish named Twitty. Next came Lorenzo Lopez with a cat, Fang. Fang scratched Lorenzo and tried to get a bite of the goldfish, Twitty. When Samantha Rissota arrived with her big shaggy dog named Crackers, Crackers immediately took off after Fang, the cat, dragging Samantha behind as she held fast to the leash. As Samantha went flying by, she accidentally knocked over Jacob Fritz and his ant farm. The ant farm broke, and thousands of ants began to crawl away. "Doc, Loretta, Steve and Darlene, Licorice, Pepper, come back!" Jacob knelt over the ants and pleaded with them to return. Just then, Fibber, Tasha Armstrong's parrot, landed next to the ants and looked at them with great interest. "Fibber!" Tasha cried and raced across the room to tackle her parrot. The parrot flew to perch on the light fixtures, and Tasha flew into Jonny McAndrew, who was carrying two pet frogs, Antony and Cleopatra. The frogs hopped away slowly and then more quickly as they realized they were being chased by Fang the cat. Fang the cat was being chased by Crackers the dog, and Lindsay Harper was trying to get her goldfish, Twitty, back into the bowl, but she was too slippery. Mrs. Wolfe was trying to remove the ants that were crawling on her when she saw Victoria Pleasant arriving with her snake, Priscilla, and Jake Jasso coming up behind Victoria with his pet monkey, Billie. Mrs. Wolfe, scratching her arms and legs, blocked the doorway, which surprised Victoria, Priscilla, Jake, and Billie. "Stop! You're too late. Pet day is over. This was the last pet day ever, and you may go home now. Try not to be late for school tomorrow!" Victoria, with Priscilla wrapped around her neck, smiled and skipped home. When Jake went to peek in the window to the classroom, he saw that Mrs. Wolfe was clapping her hands and saying, "Now class! It's short day today; you may go home now!"

Page 10 Titles and . . .
What People Are Seeing
There are many hardworking people in our part of the U.S.A., and our busy reporters set out to discover what these hard workers do for entertainment when it's time to take a break. First, we asked Dr. Lewis S. Chimney what movie he saw last weekend. This is what Dr. Chimney had to say, "As an emergency room doctor, I really don't need to see any more accidents or messy injuries, so I stay away from violent movies." Last weekend he rented *Mary Poppins*. He said that his favorite song in the movie is "Chim, Chim-Cheree." "The chimney sweeps," he added, "are the best!"
Lyle M. Sewsmith, M.D., said that he spent his one day off last week at the art museum. "I really like the Van Gogh section," Dr. Sewsmith said. His favorite Van Gogh painting is titled *Starry Night*. A plastic surgeon, Dr. Sewsmith spent a long time studying Van Gogh's self-portrait.
Mrs. D.L. Cleat, a busy school teacher, went to a sculpture garden on her way to a baseball game on Saturday. She said that she saw a version of *The Thinker*, a sculpture by Rodin. "I wish all my students would think that hard," she commented. At the ball game she sang, "Take Me out to the Ball Game," along with all the fans.
Jan L. McJet, Ph.D., a scientist at JPL, took her kids, Miranda, Mark, Jr., and Misha to see *The Magic Flute*. "It was very nice," she said, "but the youngest, Misha, got bored and started to cry." Where was Mr. McJet on this sunny Saturday? "He's at a PTA convention. We miss him!"
Jason Nurdberry, a student, said that he spent his weekend writing a story. "It's about a guy who wants to join the CIA. The only problem is that he's just 12 years old, but he's really smart and would do a great job. He spends all his time trying to prove to them how much they need him. I got the idea from an article about the CIA in *Reader's Digest*."
So it is that the very busy people around here are also busy on the weekends. What we have learned from these hard workers gives new meaning to the phrase, "Thank goodness it's Friday!" (TGIF).

Page 15 Sentences
One day, Mike and Chris were riding their skateboards at the park. When they stopped to rest, they noticed something in the bushes. "What is that?" Chris asked. Mike looked more closely. "It's furry!" Mike said. Both boys stood and stared, and then they saw it move just a little bit.
"Ohhh," Chris said, "that scared me!"
"It's a little bunny!" Mike exclaimed. Sure enough, it was a scared little brown bunny hiding in the bushes. Mike and Chris cornered it, and then Mike scooped it up. He could feel its heart beating very rapidly.
The boys walked around the park asking people if they lost a bunny. Nobody claimed it, so Mike and Chris took it home. Mike sat in a chair watching TV and held the bunny close to his chest. Chris made telephone calls to try to find out who lost the bunny. Next, they made signs and put them up around the park and in the neighborhood. The signs said, "Lost Bunny," and gave their telephone number. No one claimed the bunny.
"You can't keep it," Chris and Mike's dad said.
"Why not?" Chris asked.
"We already have a bunny cage," Mike added.
"Well, okay," Dad said, "but you'll have to give it food and water every day."
The boys were happy. They named the rabbit "George," even though it was a girl rabbit. They fed her all the vegetable scraps from the kitchen—rabbit food, cabbage, dandelions, and water. George grew to be a big fat rabbit who would sometimes visit the neighbor's yards to eat weeds and dandelions which are, to this day, her favorite foods.

Page 17 It's All Relative
1. Uncle Jorge sat on the front porch.
2. I said, "Mom, what I really want to do is stay home!"
3. My mom and my dad won't be home until 7 P.M.
4. His grandma made a quilt for his birthday.
5. My cousin and my grandma will be coming with my mom.
6. Our grandparents have a surprise for Aunt Aimee.
7. "Dear Grandma," I wrote at the top of my stationery.
8. I wish my aunt lived closer to us; she looks just like Mom.
9. Then Dad stopped and looked behind him.
10. I like to go to Grandmother Norton's house in the summer.
11. My favorite cousin is Jimmy because he makes me laugh.
12. At the wedding we saw Aunt Marsha and Cousin Brad.
13. My mom and dad are taking me to dinner after the awards assembly.
14. At the reunion I saw Aunt Edith and Uncle Jacques, and Cousins Kathy, Meredith, Hector, and Samantha.
15. For my birthday I'm inviting Cousin Sarah, Cousin Leigh, Aunt Susie, and my uncle, whose name is Mike.

Page 18 Subjects . . .
1. Shell Oil Company
2. Latin
3. algebra
4. First National Bank
5. Oak Grove Elementary School
6. European Modern Art
7. Miller Publishing House
8. World Tennis Association
9. science
10. English

Page 21 Review
1. The first day of school is exciting.
2. Freddy Wilson's frog Peepers hopped into Mrs. Woolsey's purse.
3. As I walked outside, I smelled smoke.

Capitalization and Punctuation

Answer Key (cont.)

4. In the play, Robin Hood was played by Lieutenant Bronksy.
5. The fourth Thursday in November is Thanksgiving.
6. I like Halloween best when it is on a Saturday.
7. Aunt Susan went to Yellowstone National Park.
8. Connie lives on Maple Street in Bismark, North Dakota.
9. Brazil, Argentina, and Peru are in South America.
10. The Mediterranean Sea and the Atlantic Ocean touch Spain.
11. The letter was signed, "Love always, Esther."
12. Davis Medical Center opened in January last year.
13. One of the religions practiced by many African people is Islam.
14. Italians and Germans belong to the Caucasian race.
15. Last Tuesday Ruben walked his dog Spotty down Tulip Street to Central Park.

Page 24 When and Why . . . .
Imagine reading a story that has no punctuation and no spaces, so everything runs together. How difficult would it be to communicate with others? Don't you think that would be a mess? You're right, it would be a mess. People would have so much trouble being understood, wouldn't they? Punctuation was invented to be an important part of our language system. Punctuation marks make it possible for us to manage our words and ideas. And they help the reader understand just exactly what it is that you want to say.

Page 30 End Marks
(Note: Allow for differences in interpreting some sentences. Since they are taken out of context, some students might think that an imperative sentence ought to be an exclamatory sentence or that a declarative one should be exclamatory. It is better that students think about and discuss how a sentence should be categorized than to have all their answers match these below.)

1. Oh boy, it's time for recess! exclamatory
2. I'm not sure where to go because I'm new here. declarative
3. Where do I go for recess? interrogative
4. Do you mean, "way over there where it's all sandy"? interrogative
5. Oh well, at least there are some swings over here. declarative
6. Hey, watch where you're going! exclamatory
7. Don't throw sand. imperative
8. Now that's an interesting looking ball. declarative
9. Where did you get it? interrogative
10. Be careful where you throw that thing. imperative
11. Can I play, too? interrogative
12. I'm not kidding, I really like to play. declarative
13. Oh no, there goes the bell! exclamatory
14. Okay class, let's line up. imperative
15. I really didn't get much of a chance to play, but I suppose I already had my chance when I was little; now I need to be the teacher. declarative

Page 31 Abbreviations

1. n	6. j	11. m
2. b	7. f	12. i
3. h	8. a	13. k
4. e	9. o	14. g
5. l	10. d	15. c

Page 33 Contractions
I <u>cannot</u> believe it. I wrote 25 invitations that said: "<u>You are</u> invited to a surprise party for Serena. <u>Do not</u> tell her or she <u>will not</u> come." We <u>could not</u> have the party on any day but the 18th because <u>it is</u> close to Serena's birthday, and <u>it is</u> the only day in the entire month of April <u>that is</u> free. I stamped them and said to my dog, Sugar, "<u>Let us</u> mail these before <u>it is</u> too late." You <u>will not</u> believe what happened next. It <u>must have</u> taken Sugar and me three hours just to mail the invitations after <u>I had</u> spent six hours making them because Sugar <u>must have</u> stopped at every tree. And then she barked at every bird; <u>she would</u> lie down if I tried to hurry her. Then she chased a cat up a tree, and she <u>did not</u> want to leave. <u>There have</u> been some new families <u>who have</u> moved in down the street, so Sugar wanted to sniff each of their new driveways. There <u>must have</u> been a dozen new driveways. And a huge dog came running out at us. I <u>should not</u> have run, but I <u>could not</u> help it. <u>It is</u> instinctive to run when a snarling dog appears. It <u>would have</u> eaten us both alive, or at least <u>that is</u> what I was thinking when I decided that <u>I had</u> better run. I ran, dragging Sugar at the same time because <u>she had</u> decided that <u>she would</u> save the universe from the world's meanest dog. <u>I will</u> make a long story short by telling you that while I was trying to avoid death and while Sugar was trying to save the universe, the mean dog <u>would have</u> had us both for breakfast, but all three of us ended up tangled together in a whimpering, snarling knot of fur and tasty human skin. I <u>was not</u> doing a very good job of getting out of the mess, but at least the dogs were also stuck so we <u>were not</u> going anywhere. Then I heard a voice, "<u>Who is</u> this, Fluffy? It looks like <u>we are</u> meeting our neighbors." Fluffy? I was thinking it <u>would have</u> been better to name this dog Terminator. There I was. I was covered with dog slobber and fur, and I <u>was not</u> a pretty sight. Instead of meeting a new neighbor while standing, I <u>could not</u> believe that I was saying hello on my back while one dog, which <u>should not</u> be allowed on the street, was sitting on my stomach and drooling on my face, and another dog, which <u>would not</u> ever be allowed out of the house again, was licking my leg. <u>What is</u> wrong with this picture? My very good-looking neighbor <u>must not</u> have a very interesting life because he was laughing and enjoying the whole thing.
And if that <u>were not</u> enough, when I got home my mother told me that she <u>would have</u> stopped me if <u>she had</u> known that I was mailing the invitations. I <u>had not</u> been gone for three minutes when my sister called and told my mom that <u>she had</u> decided when to have her wedding and that <u>she would</u> like me to be a bridesmaid. <u>Here is</u> the part that convinces me that <u>it is</u> not a good idea to get out of bed on some days. <u>She has</u> decided to have her wedding on the 18th— you know, the day of Serena's surprise party? <u>She has</u> already reserved the church. <u>I am</u> so embarrassed. Now <u>I will</u> need to cancel the party. And my neighbor still laughs at me every time he sees me.

Page 34 That's Mine!
1. cat's food
2. a bird's nest
3. Miguel's bike
4. Kim's store
5. David's CD player
6. my sister's book
7. my brother's skateboard
8. a baby's toys
9. the teacher's desk
10. a painter's brush
1. Nicky ran screaming into Manuel's house.
2. My dad knocked down a hornets' nest.
3. I wish I could drive my brother's car.
4. An alien ate Mariela's homework.
5. Grandpa's spaghetti is the best in the world.

Page 35 When and Where?
1. My parents bought their first home on January 13, 1976.
2. My mom was born on March 31, 1948.
3. We went to Disneyland on Tuesday, August 18, and it was really crowded!
4. My brother's birthday is November 17, 1973.
5. On Saturday, April 19, we are flying to my grandma's house.
6. I get my tonsils out on Monday, September 16, and then I can eat lots of ice cream.
7. Our puppies were born on February 14, 1997.
8. It rained cats and dogs on January 18, 1995.
9. Aliens reprogrammed my little brother on Wednesday, June 17.

© Teacher Created Materials, Inc. 47 #2329 How to Capitalize and Punctuate

Capitalization and Punctuation

Answer Key (cont.)

10. I will be a wart hog on Friday, October 31.
1. Yesterday, I met a girl from Canberra, Australia.
2. A hurricane went to shore at Acapulco, Mexico.
3. I've never been to Seattle, Washington.
4. It can get very cold in Buffalo, New York.
5. Yesterday I received e-mail from Bordeaux, France.
6. Many movie stars live in La Canada-Flintridge, California.
7. Alexandria, Virginia, is an interesting historic town.
8. You can take a great train ride in Durango, Colorado.
9. Have you been on the roller coasters in St. Louis, Missouri?
10. The mountains are really high in Vail, Colorado.

1–5: Accept appropriate responses.

Page 36 Where's My List?
1. All birds have feathers, wings, and beaks.
2. My sister is sleepy, grumpy, and clueless.
3. I would have done my homework, but I was abducted by aliens, was left in Siberia, and had to wait for the Marines to rescue me.
4. I ordered a pizza with cheese, pickles, and sliced cherries.
5. Please go to the store and get flypaper, chopsticks, and kumquats.
6. I went to the door with rollers in my hair, a mud mask on my face, and wearing my headgear.
7. My dog has brown spots, a short tail, and fuzzy feet.
8. My little brother can't go anywhere without his blanket, his stuffed duck, and his rabbit's foot key chain.
9. When I go to college I am taking a stereo, a microwave, and a treadmill.
10. For her birthday, Mindy wants some edible flowers, sparkly socks, and a pony.
1. My rabbit has long, floppy ears.
2. A large, heavy sparrow could weigh 200 pounds.
3. My teacher has a green, pointy nose.
4. My dad used to have curly, frizzy hair.
5. A friendly, playful giraffe ate all my spaghetti.

Page 38 Set It Off!
1. No, Marlene does not like being squirted in the face.
2. Christopher, how long have you been on the telephone?
3. Well, just what did you have in mind?
4. Sure, Laura, I'd love another jelly donut.
5. My brother, the world's scariest boy, likes escargot.
6. The plane we are taking, a 747, will have plenty of room.
7. You realize, of course, that you will not be allowed out of the house in that outfit.
8. My orthodontist, Dr. Baugh, decorated his office for Halloween.
9. All right, if that's what you think, let's just eat all of the chocolate.
10. In the future, we will be able to speak to our computers.
11. No kidding, you went rock climbing?
12. We went to Bouquet Canyon, a canyon near Valencia, to attend a harvest festival.
13. You could read, for example, some books about the historical period in which your novel takes place.
14. For Valentine's Day, my dad gave me two pounds of my favorite treat, candy corn.
15. I don't care what you think, I'm going to go back there and help that little boy.

Page 40 May I Quote You?
1. "What is that bizarre thing upon your head? It looks like an octopus," said Mr. Grimmy.
"What is that bizarre thing upon your head? It looks like and octopus," said Mr. Grimmy.
2. The teacher told the students to read the story, "The Raven," by Friday.
title
3. I call my sister "Idget," but I have no idea why.
4. "Hey!" Jacques shouted, "Didn't you hear the coach? He said, 'Stop when you get to the fence!'"
a quote within a quote
5. "And then I will cover you with fragrant rose petals," Mama said, "and sing a lullaby."
6. I found a book that said, "Dinosaurs may be more closely related to birds than to lizards."
7. We have family nicknames, and my brother's is "Greasy Bear."
special words, phrases
8. "Did you hear what Nicole said?" Amy asked us. "She said, 'You guys are just too chicken to try it.' She doesn't know what she is talking about!"
9. I thought you would be too "cool" to go on the merry-go-round with me.
10. She watched *Somewhere in Time* so many times she wore out the tape.
11. My brother always talks in his sleep. Last night he said, "Hurry and purple it before the snails get it!"
exact words
12. After we watched *Twister* we couldn't stop watching the clouds.
title
13. "Come with us," Dad said, "and we can stop for ice cream on the way."
14. I need to find the root word for "transient."
15. Mom says we shouldn't say "Where's he at?" because it is not proper English.
special word, phrase

Page 41 . . . Little Marks?
Accept appropriate responses.

Page 43 Review
Our class went on a very special field trip. We saved up money from newspapers and recycling aluminum cans until we had enough for a group rate to Disneyland. Isn't that exciting?
We also had to save up enough for the bus, which wasn't too expensive. When the day finally came, we were so excited. We sang songs like "Bingo" and "The Ants Go Marching In" all the way there. The bus driver said he was going to go crazy, but he was just kidding because he was also going to Disneyland, and he was happy about that.
When we got there, Marisa said, "I see Space Mountain!" Then Luke said, "I see the Matterhorn Mountain!" Then Hector said, "I see Splash Mountain!" And, of course, then Olivia said, "I see Thunder Mountain!"
The bus driver said maybe they should call it "Mountainland" instead. Nobody said anything because just then we all saw the monorail go by. "I want to go on the monorail," Cassie said, but Mrs. Martinez said that we had to go through the entrance first.
After we went through the entrance, everybody forgot about the monorail. We were divided into groups so we could go wherever our group wanted to go, and we could join with other groups, too, whenever we wanted to. Because we all wore bright orange shirts, it wouldn't be too hard to find each other. Mrs. Martinez took a group, and so did Mr. Rawlings, Ms. White, Mrs. Hojito, and Bill, the bus driver. Guess what? I was in Bill-the-bus-driver's group! I'll never forget this day; our group had more fun than any other group because Bill went on all the rides with us, and he didn't complain at all. In fact, he said, "I'm having too much fun!" Isn't that great? Bill-the-bus-driver even rode the bobsleds with us, and he went on the Autopia, too. He didn't get sick on Dumbo or the merry-go-round, and he even went on Splash Mountain, Thunder Mountain, and Space Mountain, On Indiana Jones, he covered his eyes when a snake hissed at him, and on the Jungle Cruise he shrieked when a hippopotamus blew water on him. He made us all laugh all the time. At the very end, Bill-the-bus-driver got motion sickness on the teacups. Someone was coming to pick him up and to bring a new bus driver. That meant we got to go back into Disneyland for one more hour! We felt sorry for Bill, but we were so glad to have another hour!